A CHAPLAIN'S PERSPECTIVE

— ON THE —

2020-2021 PANDEMIC

Tragedy, Resilience, Hope

JOHN RUIZ

ISBN
978-1-954932-98-2 (Paperback)
978-1-954932-97-5 (eBook)

To all the healthcare heroes
and support staff. You make a positive
impact in the lives of others every day.

Table of Contents

Introduction

I began these writings on Easter Sunday 2020. At that time, there was much uncertainty and fear surrounding the Coronavirus and no one knew what to expect during a pandemic. It quickly became apparent that one of the truths of a worldwide pandemic is everyone will have a unique experience, their own personal story of the pandemic. The reflections that follow draw upon those experiences and seek to produce a picture of life, challenge and hope at the bedside as a hospital chaplain in a large hospital.

Initially, the reflections seemed to be a way of centering and purging thoughts and emotions. As time went by, I began to realize the importance of these writings on a personal level. As I shared them at both a hospital and church level, the feedback I received was very positive, as people said they were beneficial and meaningful. I hope that these reflections of a chaplain during the 2020-2021 pandemic serve as a helpful and healing way of processing your own experience of the pandemic.

Easter 2020

I work as a chaplain at a large 300+ bed hospital in Columbus, Ohio. My primary assignment is the Emergency Department where we average around 2500 traumas and between 80,000-90,000 patient visits a year. In this environment you never know what the next moment might look like, as the hospital staff never knows the next need that might enter the door. It is part of the job. It is part of the unique experience of the emergency department.

However, the coronavirus is different. As I write these words 110,005 people around the world have died as a result of this virus.[1] I am sure when I am finished with these words the number will be higher. In the United States 20,580 people have died and in my own state, 247 people have lost their lives.[2] I have personally been with families that have lost a loved one to the disease.

The coronavirus changed things in terrifying ways, yet the subsequent human response has been nothing less than inspiring. Let me explain. As hospital employees, we never know what may come in next into an emergency department, but we

[1] Worldometers.info.coronavirus
[2] Ibid

also hold a quiet confidence. All staff members have trained extensively, and we trust our training. Over time we learn to trust your teammates and what each person brings to the team.

For a time, the coronavirus took this confidence away and brought a level of fear to the medical and support staff. As horrendous the car accident can be, we did not feel that we might be putting ourselves and the ones we love at risk.

I remember Friday, March 27 very well. It was the first day we had a COVID+ patient in the hospital. In fact, before the shift ended, we had three COVID+ patients in the hospital. At one point the emergency department had ten suspected patients. As a hospital we had prepared six rooms in the emergency department for COVID+ patients and we had thirty-two beds in the main hospital staffed and ready to receive those patients.

Obviously at this moment we felt behind the curve, but the courage and resolve of the team was incredible. Staff who were working directly in patient rooms were able to gown appropriately. Observing nurses, PCAs (Patient Care Assistants), respiratory therapists, pharmacists and doctors enter these rooms again and again is something I will never forget. Watching the team perform CPR on a suspected COVID+ patient, with all the potential threats involved to themselves and to those they love has given me a new perspective on sacrificial love. The sacrificial love revealed to the world through the life, death and resurrection of Jesus.

On this Friday afternoon, the hospital support staff including unit coordinators, registration, social workers, transportation, dietitian, maintenance, house cleaning and chaplains had not yet been given PPE (Personal Protective Equipment). There simply was not enough PPE to go around. Everyone knew the risk could be literally in the air as patient after patient was brought by EMS. No matter how prepared any ER is, it is impossible to fully isolate a patient while wheeling them through the emergency department to their equipped room where the gowned team awaits their arrival.

And yet everyone stayed, doing their jobs and attempting to do their part. When I returned to work the next Monday the resilient and resourceful upper-management team had acted, and we had nearly fifteen rooms in the emergency department that had been modified by brave construction workers for COVID+ patients. Over the course of the weekend our hospital capacity had increased to forty-eight rooms prepared to receive COVID+ patients.

This expansion capacity has continued and when I left work on Thursday, April 9, we had thirty emergency department beds ready and ninety-six floor beds. For the past week we have had between twelve to twenty COVID+ patients admitted to the hospital. Another thirty to forty patients were admitted and waiting for test results leaving us with thirty to forty beds available. The hospital administration is always trying to stay ahead of the curve and plans are in place to expand to 128 rooms assigned for COVID+ patients if needed.

What is the role of the chaplain during this pandemic and how has it changed from pre-pandemic days? The chaplain's role can be summarized in three ways: Prayer, Presence and Representatives of Hope.

I am very fortunate to work in a hospital system that allows an overhead prayer. Each Monday morning, I have prayed this prayer.

> *To everything there is a Season…* (Ecclesiastes 3:1a)

> Oh, good and gracious God, Our Heavenly Father. So much of life has changed for each of us in the recent past and today we face challenges that we could not have imagined.

> Be with us dear God. Be with us in our frustrations and fears. Be with us whenever we might feel overwhelmed and fatigued. Be with us each day as we do the best, we possibly can for those we serve and for each other. Be with us in our weeping and in our resiliency.

> Bless those Heavenly Father that we love and carry with us in our minds and in our hearts. Give us strength and courage. Fill us with compassion and give us the wisdom to know when it is time to be still and allow You to refresh our souls so we can continue to face the challenges before us rooted in Your truth and hope.

For there is a time for every season. A time to weep and a time to laugh. Lead us, Oh God, to the time of laughter once again. In Your Holy name we pray. Amen.

As a spiritual care department, we attempt to provide overhead prayer as often as possible. We have been asked many times to pray with individual staff or teams. The overhead prayer can reach the most people and staff reaction has been plentiful and positive. One chaplain took it upon herself to sanitize and handout to staff over a hundred tokens with either a dove on one side and the word "peace" on the reverse or an angel on one side and the word "faith" on the opposite side. Many staff members seemed to draw great strength from these tokens, as having something tangible to simply hold onto is centering for them in the midst of uncertainty. An amazing Nigerian priest and hospital chaplain received special permission from the bishop to gown and enter the room of COVID+ Catholic patients to administer the sacraments including confession, communion and Anointing of the Sick.

Presence is a huge part of the ministry of a chaplain; being a compassionate presence who can keep your head when frequently the people around you cannot, is the beginning point of every encounter with patients and families. Holding a patient's hand, extending a kind touch, a caring smile, an empathetic ear, or a knowing and warm look in the eye are invaluable tools a chaplain uses every day. However, these tools are very limited when patients are in isolation and families are unable to enter the hospital and visit their loved one.

Isolation presents a new and difficult challenge and reminds us how true it is that God made us to be in relationship. Being in relationship with other people and with God is what it means to be fully human.

Ministering in these situations is done primarily through phone and with families. On occasion a chaplain may be able to talk on the phone with a patient, but most patients are too sick and exhausted to talk in this way. There are times when families have requested a prayer for a loved one and the chaplain simply stands outside the room and prays. Prayer is a very powerful gift God has given us and not even a virus, not even a pandemic, can take that away!

Further, the chaplains try and track potential COVID patients that have tested negative and moved to another part of the hospital. Families are still not allowed to visit, and the chaplain visit is usually most welcomed by the patient as they begin to process and emerge from their isolation. Human contact and an empathetic ear can be very healing. Additionally, the presence of the chaplain continues in all areas of the hospital that continue to function in non-COVID ways; heart attacks, strokes, car accidents, violence, palliative care, general sickness, deaths and births continue, and the chaplain seeks to meet these needs as well.

Finally, the chaplain is a representative of hope. At no time in my ministry has this been truer. Simply walking through the hospital can take hours and be exhausting as we are stopped for small talk and not so small talk. You can sense and feel people drawing energy and hope out of you. It's hard to explain, yet very, very real.

Today is Easter and it feels very strange not to be in church. Yet today is still Easter! A day where we celebrate the resurrection of Christ. A day where we ponder the mystery of the empty tomb and the victory of Resurrection Hope!

Tomorrow at 7am, I will be back at the hospital and I have no idea what will await me. But what I do know, rooted in truth and grace, is that an amazing team throughout the hospital embodying sacrificial love will await me. I do know that God's power in prayer and presence awaits me. And I do know the truth of hope, for hope is not rooted in a human feeling but rather is known in a Risen Savior! Amen.

"He leads me beside still waters"

The last time I had a chance to write was Easter morning and it is hard to believe all that has happened in the past nine weeks. The COVID-19 virus has had an impact on so many facets of life.

I am writing this reflection on June 10th and as of today over 400,000 people around the world have died.[3] In the past week we passed 110,000 deaths in the United States.[4] My home state of Ohio passed 2400 deaths due to COVID-19.[5] The hospital where I work is nearing thirty and I have personally been the chaplain with ten families who have lost a loved one to the virus. The ages of these patients were between forty-seven and seventy-nine. I am fifty-five and am fortunate to have living parents. These ages do not seem old to me.

In the midst of this, the chaplain's role is to provide and represent insights found in our unique position in the hospital. Having this in mind, let me briefly explain that role.

A chaplain is to be a compassionate presence who can keep their head when frequently the people around them cannot.

3   Worldometers.info.coronavirus

4   Ibid

5   Ibid

This is the beginning point of every encounter with patients, families and staff and it needs to happen 100% of the time.

There are times when being a compassionate presence who can keep their head is all that happens within a patient visit or family encounter and that action can be a very effective chaplain encounter. At the same time, the chaplain is trained to assess and bring forth whatever has given that person or family hope, meaning and strength in the past. To say it another way, the chaplain journeys and encourages the person or family to access within themselves whatever it is that has given their lives hope, meaning and strength. Finally, and for some this is the hardest part, the chaplain must be open and respectful to how that person or family answers that question.

On occasion the chaplain is called upon to add insights from their own professional and theological training. In my situation, I am a Christian pastor, therefore the lens by which I seek to view life is the lens of "grace and truth" (1:17b).

How does the lens of grace and truth influence and inform our understanding of this pandemic?

First, it provides a solid perspective. I remember very well the first day the Center for Disease Control (CDC) posted causality projections for the United States. This was posted before any political or media spin occurred. On this day everything in the hospital changed. In fact, everything in the nation seemed to change on a dime.

The initial CDC projection in March 2020 was 200,000 to 1.7 million deaths in the United States with a medium of

480,000 deaths.[6] Clearly, without being said, the potential for millions of deaths worldwide could be assumed.

Rooted in this foundation of truth, we are equipped to join others in their personal grief and in the mourning of human loss unprecedented in my lifetime. We are also positioned to recognize and celebrate the incredible human effort in joining together for each other. Millions and millions of individual choices and sacrifices have made a tremendous difference; 110,000 deaths are not 200,000 or 480,000 or 1.7 million. Worldwide 400,000+ have died and this is not millions. Human decisions and sacrifices have made a difference!

Encouraging others to properly mourn and acknowledging sacrifices made together for each other (often-times people who live in distant areas of the world who we will never meet face to face) is rooted in grace and truth. Second, the virus has a way of intruding into our lives slowly and methodically. At one time it was occurring "over there". Then it was closer, and the cities being impacted were in the USA, then the state of Ohio and on March 27 my own hospital. Since that time, we have had between twenty-five to thirty-five COVID+ patients daily. Most have recovered. A growing number have died.

Two of my assigned units (thirty-two beds) are assigned for COVID+ patients only. Watching these teams of professionals who are working with these patients has been amazing. Initially, there was anxiety mixed with fear met with a sense of professionalism and resolve. As the weeks have passed, the

---

[6] Worst-Case Estimates for U.S. Coronavirus Deaths: March 13, 2020, The New York Times, Sheri Fink.

abnormal has gradually become normal as the same individuals put on their gear and enter COVID+ rooms in an almost routine way. And this routine of abnormality creates new challenges.

I remember the first time a healthcare worker from another facility was treated as a patient on the unit. The virus crept closer and the reality of the daily risks being made got closer. The first time I knew someone who was quarantined for being COVID+; the virus got closer. The first family who lost a loved one; the virus got closer. Fortunately, as I write these words, I have not personally lost someone to the virus.

Each time the virus gets closer, we are challenged to dig deep within ourselves and bring forth whatever it is that has given our lives hope, meaning and strength.

Is it any wonder to read about healthcare professionals who simply could not cope with the stress, loss and continued challenges the virus brings? If a person answers the question of hope, meaning and strength in a way that is rooted in my own professional skills, the quality of the team I work with and my personal resolve I might be in trouble.

The reality is the number of people who cannot be saved medically is staggering and living within this harsh truth is extremely difficult.

The reality is hundreds of medical professionals around the world have died from contracting the disease as they served others. One can only imagine the devastating impact if this is one of my teammates.

The reality is there are times when people are on breathing machines for weeks and months. What toll might this take on the medical professionals who begin questioning their own skills?

What can the chaplain offer?

Over the weeks the overhead morning prayer has changed to try and meet the current moment. Now, every Monday morning the prayer heard throughout the hospital reads:

> *The Lord is my shepherd I shall not want. He makes me lie down in green pastures: He leads me beside still waters. He restores my soul.* (Psalm 23:1-2)

O loving and Creator God, our Heavenly Father.
So much has happened in the recent past and for the
past few months we have faced challenges that would
have been unimaginable but a short time ago.

We give you thanks, O God, for leading us through
this crisis; for giving us resiliency and hope.

And today we add to our prayers a sense of comfort
to all who have lost a loved one; a sense of peace
and resolve for all of us as we try and do our best
during this pandemic for our patients, each other, our
families and for people throughout the world we may
never meet face to face. And a sense of wisdom.

Oh, Good Shepherd, it is becoming clear that the challenges
we are facing will continue to be with us for some time.

Give us the wisdom to know our human frailties and
limitations so that we know when it is time to be still
by still waters and allow You to restore our souls.

Continue to lead us to a time of laughter.
For there is a time for every season... (Ecclesiastes 3:1)

What is it that gives your life hope, meaning and strength
and how might you encourage and assist others in accessing
hope, meaning and strength in themselves?

For me, hope, meaning and strength are found in the One
who is the embodiment of grace and truth; Jesus. Through this
I find great comfort in God my Shepherd who leads me beside
still waters and restores my soul (Psalm 23:1-2). God, who is
faithful at all times and in all places in this life and in the life
to come (Psalm 23 and Romans 8:31-35 and 37-39).

Be blessed.

It's Been Three Months

It's been three months. It is hard to believe it has only been three months since we had the first COVID+ patient in the hospital. March 27th the coronavirus pandemic became real and for nearly two months we have consistently had between twenty-five to thirty-five COVID+ patients in Intensive Care beds in our hospital. As I write today marks exactly three months.

I work at a large 300 bed hospital in Columbus, Ohio. My primary assignment is the Emergency department where we average 2500 trauma cases and between 80,000-90,000 patient visits a year. I also cover assigned units. During the pandemic two of my units (thirty-two beds) have been assigned to only treat COVID+ patients. For myself, and the incredible team I work with the coronavirus is a very real part of every day.

The beginning point of every chaplain encounter with patients, families and staff is to be a compassionate presence who can keep your head when frequently the people around you cannot. In this way, a chaplain becomes acutely aware that there are times when the reality of the moment can be too much, and a patient or family can be overwhelmed with emotion and the ability to think is unattainable. Emotion can overload the cognitive brain; this can occur in times of crisis such as a new and very difficult diagnosis or the death of a loved one.

In the hospital I work the chaplain is called into these situations to be a calming, comforting, compassionate presence who can simply be with people as they absorb the emotions of the moment and are able to think more clearly. There are times a person's cognitive brain can be "off- line" for minutes. At times this struggle can last for hours and on occasion, days. In each of these cases the chaplain seeks to journey with people until they can fully process, think with clarity and begin to envision a "new normal," as difficult as that new normal might be.

The ferocity of the virus and the fear, frustration, and grief that it has brought to our collective "new normal" has created times when it is difficult to think clearly. You can even say that there are times when collectively it is hard to fully process the moment and think rationally.

Let me give an example: on June 11, 2020, Dr. Amy Acton, the Ohio Health Director resigned, largely due to many in the public raising criticisms and concerns against her leadership. Obviously, the virus and the collective human response has been a challenge economically for everyone and for some, a devastating reality.

At the same time, when we stop and think of the reason behind all the sacrifices made, we recall that the purpose for businesses closing, the loss of jobs and the stay at home guidelines was to flatten the curve so that the medical institutions were not overwhelmed by a tsunami of COVID+ patients. It was feared this type of flood could temporarily break the medical capabilities of a community, city or state which would lead to a huge surge of death and despair.

From my vantage point as a hospital chaplain, we were close to the breaking point. For a month or so we were very close to being overwhelmed. And the reality is we were not! We have always had enough beds, necessary medical equipment to take care of COVID+ patients and available staff to care for all the patients throughout the hospital.

In this way, the fact that Dr. Acton resigned on June 11, 2020 becomes puzzling for the stated goal of flattening the curve worked! And by flattening the curve we have collectively saved thousands of lives in the great state of Ohio!

Growing up in Ohio it comes naturally to compete with "that state up north"; football, basketball, chess, it does not matter. Beating MICHIGAN always feels good. So, lets compare the Ohio response to the Michigan response and the coronavirus.

Michigan has the tenth largest population 9,986,857 and is the eleventh largest state with 96, 713 square miles in the United States.[7] Ohio has the seventh largest population 11,689,100 and is the 34th largest state with 44,825 square miles.[8]

Logic would conclude that Ohio would experience more death due to the coronavirus than Michigan. Did this happen?

---

[7]   United States Census Bureau. Retrieved February 8, 2020. Census 2000 Geography Glossary, U.S. Census Bureau.

[8]   United States Census Bureau. Retrieved February 8, 2020. Census 2000 Geography Glossary, U.S. Census Bureau.

The truth revealed can be healing and empowering. To date Ohio has lost 2795 precious souls which correlates to 239 deaths per million.[9] In the same period, Michigan has experienced 6133 deaths which correlates to 614 deaths per million.[10]

Allow that to sink in and say a prayer. Thank a fellow Ohioan you have never met. The sacrifices made for each other have made an incredible difference!

This truth is reinforced when we compare Ohio to Pennsylvania, another neighboring mid-western state. Pennsylvania has the fifth largest population 12,801,989 and is the 33rd largest state with 46,054 square miles.[11] In Pennsylvania 6616 people have died of the coronavirus which correlates to 517 deaths per million.[12]

Logic would say we give a huge "Thank You" to Dr. Amy Acton and the state leadership that has guided us this far.

Prayer continues to be a tangible practice the chaplain can model to patients, families and staff. Prayer that reflects the truth that we are not alone, and that God is with us in the midst of it all. And once again the Monday morning prayer has changed to speak to the challenges of the day.

---

[9] Worldometers.info.coronavirus

[10] Ibid

[11] United States Census Bureau. Retrieved February 8, 2020. Census 2000 Geography Glossary, U.S. Census Bureau.

[12] Worldometers.info.coronavirus

God is the same, yesterday, today and forever (Hebrews 13:8).

Oh, good and gracious God, we give You thanks for the gift of this beautiful day and all the possibility it brings

At the same time there is so much turmoil in our world and communities; we are experiencing the first worldwide pandemic of our lifetimes which has brought enormous stress, death and grief. We are living through a time of social strife seeking to reflect a growing understanding of justice and praying this occurs in peaceful ways worthy of the Prince of peace.

In times of such anger, confusion, sacrifice and possibility it is good to re-center ourselves in grace and truth.

God is the same yesterday, today and forever.

Be with us, Oh God, throughout all the challenges this day may bring and within all the anger, grief, confusion, sacrifice and possibility of this time.

Continue to guide us, Oh God, and give us the wisdom to draw upon Your guidance. For there is a time for every season under heaven.

Continue to lead us to a time of peace and laughter.

In Your precious name we pray.

Amen

The Journey Continues

"He has told you, O man, what is good; and what does the Lord require of you but to do justice, and love kindness, and walk humbly with your God? (Micah 6:8)

Working in the hospital and especially on my assigned COVID+ units, the pandemic continues to be at the center of our thoughts and daily conversations. At the same time, life continues and for many, other challenges have taken priority and the pandemic has drifted to the background.

In the United States we are seeking to reflect a growing understanding of justice. We are seeking to assure that justice and the right to live and dream is known by all members of our society.

There are times this social strife that is seeking growth and change has happened peacefully and other times, protests have become violent. These are challenging times.

What perspective can a hospital chaplain bring to the Black Lives Matter cry of the moment?

First, a re-centering on the role of religion. The great Nigerian thinker Francis Cardinal Arinze said it this way,

"Human life is sacred. It must be protected. We have no right to kill ourselves or to kill innocent people. While self-defense is a right and justifiable, it has to be kept in due limits. Justice, peace, tranquility in the world are built on the pillars of respect for the fundamental rights of other people, especially their right to life, religious freedom, and free exercise of political, economic, and cultural rights. Economic and political development of people is also an obligatory road to peace. If people are illiterate, underdeveloped, oppressed and repressed, then justice and peace are rendered more difficult. Violence, terrorism, the taking of human lives and the destruction of property are condemned by all genuine religions. They are opposed to love of God and neighbor. No matter the problems and challenges to be faced, these violent roads are the wrong ones. Solutions in line with respect for God and humanity have to be sought, no matter how difficult and long-term they may be. All religions are bound to help their followers to engage in reflections such as these."[13]

Second, in support of equality, the advancement of civil rights and recognizing the increased challenges and restrictions both seen and unseen within African American communities and especially among young African American men, I am left to wonder about the challenge of change. And, as we seek to broaden our collective vision, I ask a question rooted from chaplaincy encounters at the bedside, "If Black Lives Matter

---

[13] Francis Cardinal Arinze, *Religions for Peace: A Call for Solidarity to the religions of the World* (Doubleday a division of Random House, Inc.: New York, New York) 2002, p. vii.

then would it not be logical to also say that Unborn Black Lives Matter?"

The most difficult visits for me occur in Labor and Delivery and the Neonatal Intensive Care Unit of the hospital. These visits drain me emotionally and I am continually amazed by the heroic teams of professionals called to work in these units day after day. Labor and Delivery and the Neonatal units are for the most part the happiest areas of the hospital full of new lives, but at other times, they are the saddest units in the hospital. The sadness and intense grief seem to fill the hallways and enter the hearts of all associated with the death of a baby.

On eighteen occasions I have been called by family to the room of a newborn who will not live long on this earth with the request to baptize their child. I am going to give more detail to one of these situations.

A woman went into spontaneous delivery. There was nothing the medical team could do to stop it. The baby had a heartbeat, but the gestational age was only nineteen weeks and three days. Therefore, it was known that the baby would not survive. Everyone believed medically that the child would be a stillborn. Family was at her bedside and waited with heavy hearts.

Finally, he was born, barely over a pound and breathing! No one expected him to be breathing. Nurses laid him on his mother's breast, and she swaddled him. She gazed at him and loved him. Family members gathered around and surrounded mom and her baby with love.

At some point the family requested that I baptize the baby. We gathered around the bedside. Mom continued to hold her son and using two fingers I baptized him, and we prayed to God.

He was with us, never leaving his mother's arms, for 1 hour and 48 minutes. In that brief amount of time he changed the world. He inspired so much love. He permanently impacted the lives of those blessed to see him and the one who literally held him during every moment he had on earth. His life mattered!

A Barge Boat

Jesus said, "I am the Way, the Truth and the Life."
(John 14:6a)

As an Emergency Department chaplain who also covers COVID+ intensive care units (thirty-two beds). I am called to serve in crisis ministry situations several times a day. In this way, I am frequently present in times of pain, confusion, loss and death. Elisabeth Kubler-Ross and her stages of grief theory continues to provide a valid starting point when understanding and being with those experiencing loss and grief. Today it is commonly understood that for most, the grief journey is not linear (simply one stage to the next) but rather more accurately describes the emotions felt in the "pool of grief", and these emotions are then experienced in a more haphazard manner. Kubler-Ross identified the emotions of denial, anger, bargaining, depression, and acceptance within the grief journey.

Looking at society from a chaplain's perspective it is easy to identify these stages of grief being experienced at societal levels. There continues to be a debate around wearing masks and those who seem to have an attitude of being "un-threatened" by the pandemic. We continue to see people in large group settings and those who do not wear masks, these actions can be understood as forms of denial.

Random acts of anger and violence seem to be on the rise. People are experiencing new stressors; many are separated from loved ones due to COVID. Many are experiencing financial difficulties and even devastation.

We are seeing the effects of the pandemic as many in our community are experiencing signs of depression including feeling overwhelmed, helpless, hostile or simply trying to escape the reality of the moment. Sadly, last weekend, the city of Columbus experienced a spike in overdose admissions and death. My own hospital was part of these very difficult situations.

Last Tuesday, we experienced a new hospital record for psych patients boarded in the Emergency Department. These people recognize that something is not right, and they need help. Everyone acknowledges that boarding these patients is only providing a band-aid but like most cities there is a terrible lack of beds for patients experiencing psychological issues. Keeping individuals safe (even for a short time) is better than having them on the streets. If a person is deemed a threat to self or others, they can be boarded for seventy-two hours. In some situations, the patient is with us for hours, a day or until the patient believes they are well enough to re-enter life. If deemed, they are not a threat to self or others they are able to sign themselves out of the hospital. Last Tuesday, in a twenty-four-hour period our hospital saw thirty-one boarded patients.

There is a growing sense of frustration as more and more people move to acceptance that regardless of what we do, regardless of the successes and sacrifices, regardless of the mixed messages from those in leadership, the reality is that at some point in late July or early August we will reach 150,000 people in the United States who have died from COVID-19. There is so much grief being experienced by so many people within our society and throughout the world.

How do we navigate through these turbulent, chaotic and difficult times?

Jesus said, *"I am the Way, the Truth and the Life"* (John 14a).

Several years ago, I was serving three small churches along the Ohio River. I found the river to be beautiful and frequently my black lab, Mandy, and I would go to the river. I would sit on a rock and she would play in the water.

One day I was watching a huge barge approaching. I watched for a while and then a "light bulb" went off in my head. Something was pushing the barge! I grew up hearing stories of tugboats. But this was different. The barge boat was being pushed.

Needless to say, the River Pilots who were part of the church got a good laugh! Then they explained why you must push the barge and not tug the barge to navigate the river. If you are tugging, then the pilot is frequently looking backwards, and you would quickly get stuck in the mud if you are looking backwards while navigating the Ohio River.

Pushing the barge means the pilot has their vision forward. Therefore, they can navigate the twists and turns experienced in their journey.

Jesus, who is the Way, can be the focal point in our forward journey. This focal point, like the North Star, helps us navigate.

Jesus, who is the Truth, allows us to be fully present in the truth of the moment, as difficult as that moment may be. Therefore, those who seek to dwell in the *Truth* are also able to dwell in another person's truth of denial, anger, bargaining, depression and acceptance. Having company in these emotions can be healing and comforting. At times, a chaplain can even begin to travel with that person as they begin the emotional journey of hope, joy and life.

Jesus is the Life, for as much as death is around us and is more a part of our conscious daily thoughts, life wins! Life continues, babies are born, new dreams come into focus, Jesus is with us and Loves wins!

Reflecting Beside Still Waters

By recognizing death, we are able to stand in truth. Standing in truth we can celebrate life and recognize the beauty of sacrificial love.

On October 5, 2020 the United States passed 210,000 deaths attributed to coronavirus. This was not unexpected as the daily death toll continued to rise and as human beings, we could only resolve ourselves to grieve and continue to persevere.

It has been a difficult year, and I decided to pause and reflect on the significance of the moment and the sacrifices willingly made for the benefit of others.

Throughout the pandemic, I have turned to the website MEDPAGETODAY: Honoring U.S. Healthcare Workers Who Died from the Coronavirus. The webpage is updated as needed. When I go to the site, I reflect upon the acts of courage, professionalism and kindness given by healthcare workers throughout the world and in the United States.

On this early fall day, I took the time to note the various healthcare fields where a healthcare worker has died. My first reaction was the stunning truth that the pandemic knows no boundaries. The healthcare fields impacted included nurses, doctors, nurse practitioners, mental health technicians, MRI technicians, nursing assistants, anesthesiologists, general surgeons, mammogram technologists, speech pathologists, physicians' assistants, nursing home aides, pediatric intensive care nurses, radiological technicians, clinical interpreters, phlebotomists, EKG technologists, OB/GYN physicians, radiologists and respiratory therapists.

According to the CDC, around 740 healthcare workers have died from coronavirus. Each individual willingly chose to go to work in an effort to provide care and comfort to others in their time of need. None of these individuals planned on contracting the disease. At the same time, everyone knew they were putting themselves at risk. And they chose day after day to go to work and serve others anyway. This is a message of *Sacrificial Love!*

In the flurry of this chaotic and scary year, have we taken time to hear their witness of sacrificial love?

It's there if we take the time to listen. It's there to bring hope in times of grief and pain. It's there to remind us that life can be beautiful!

A second thought occurred when I noticed the number of healthcare professionals not included by MEDPAGETODAY. It would be almost impossible to realize and recognize the various services performed by healthcare workers and individual citizens daily. At the same time, my mind wandered to paramedics, emergency medical providers, ambulance drivers, police officers, emergency medical technicians, med flight staff, unit coordinators, registration workers, hospital maintenance workers, house cleaning staff, supply and distribution personnel, in hospital transportation employees, hospital security workers, patient care assistants, administrative leadership, food services staff, social workers, chaplains and others I am sure I have forgotten. It is an incredible team of professionals, each day doing their part and each knowingly and willingly putting themselves at risk day after day.

When days get heavy and I get down, I am blessed to be inspired by the gift of sacrificial love. My wife is a nurse and my oldest son is a paramedic. I get to come to work and be surrounded by the most amazing friends and colleagues living out sacrificial love. While the pandemic has brought out much grief, anger and despair, at the same time, there are times when it has also revealed what is best in each other, displayed in our love of neighbor.

Fighting Fatigue

It has been nearly seven months since we had our first confirmed COVID+ patient in the hospital. That day stands out in my memory, March 27, 2020 to be exact. It has been quite a journey so far.

One of the things I have done since the beginning of the pandemic has been to walk the COVID+ halls at least twice a week. During these walks, I like to check in with staff to get a sense of morale, and provide an attentive ear, or words of encouragement. I talk with staff to determine especially difficult situations that might be occurring and then follow-up with family to provide support as needed. I often say a quiet prayer for the patients, families and staff. In addition, I count the number of COVID+ patients and those COVID+ patients currently on a breathing machine.

As a chaplain it is important to model faith, hope and endurance to other staff. This is grounded in the starting position of every chaplain encounter; being a compassionate presence who can keep your head when often the people around you cannot.

One of the ways a person can keep their head in difficult situations is to seek a broader perspective and even a perspective that can reasonably anticipate future behavior and events. Walking the COVID+ halls has given an avenue for these kinds of perspectives. It is the reason for this meditation, "Fighting Fatigue".

A reality for all persons in the healthcare world in these days is the necessity to reach down deep and simply do what is needed during this pandemic. In my own little corner of the world it has meant chaplains working additional hours and various shifts as budget cuts have been made, requiring staffing changes. These staffing cuts have occurred throughout the hospital (and I am sure are occurring in many healthcare systems) because of the very difficult financial realities healthcare facilities are experiencing throughout the country due to the pandemic.

As I write this meditation, I am working my sixteenth night shift this fall. I had thought working night shifts was part of my past. It was a position I worked for three years at a younger age. But all chaplains have stepped up to cover night shifts as needed. Working as a team is one of the ways we support each other and journey through the challenges of the day together.

As I walked the COVID+ halls for nearly four months, there would be twenty-five to forty patients on the units. Many of them were on breathing machines (or "vented"). Then we had a period when the number began to lower. For the past few weeks an entire hallway with sixteen beds ready to receive patients has been blocked. There has not been a need to use these beds. At one point there were only nine COVID+ patients in the hospital. Two of these patients were on a vent.

Tonight, walking the halls and listening, there is a growing sense that things are changing again. This observation alerted me to the importance of preparing oneself, friends, families and colleagues for additional challenges in the future. Tonight, walking the COVID+ hallways I counted twenty-eight COVID+ patients. Three of these patients are on vents. Staff are wondering if, or when the sixteen-bed blocked unit will be re-opened and if that will be enough.

One of the most difficult things to do for those in healing professions is to listen to your own advice. How many times have you heard that nurses and doctors make the worst patients? Or pastors and chaplains are said to be really good at caring for the needs of others and really bad at caring for their own needs.

In this way, and in the spirit of modeling, I am going to try and follow the insights of chaplaincy and an essential component of what that means. During a spiritual care encounter where you are a compassionate presence who can keep your head when frequently the people around you cannot, the chaplain is also assessing the situation to try and bring forth in those you are serving whatever has given their lives hope, meaning and strength in previous times.

Following this train of thought, I must admit that the Bible, biblical truths, personal experience and "living realities" have given my life hope, meaning and strength. In my faith tradition, a "living reality" occurs when a biblical truth intersects with one's personal life. That intersection then creates a new way of looking at and experiencing the world, and events that may be occurring in one's life. A few examples: some may talk about the experience of a peace that passes understanding (Philippians 4:7), or a moment of unspeakable joy (Luke 1:44), or a time of endurance and hope (Romans 5:4), or a time of hearing God as a whisper in the wind (I Kings 19:12b), or a Damascus road conversion experience (Acts 9:1-22). Others might recall a time of unexpected forgiveness and new-life (John 7:53-8:11), or a time of unmerited love, which results in healing and wholeness (Luke 7:36-50), or a time for every season under heaven (Ecclesiastes 3:1).

I have a great job, and these are some of the living realities that I have heard others explain to me over my twenty-five years in ministry. Further, I have been blessed to have a few times in my own life when a biblical truth intersected with personal experience and then created a living reality.

Several years ago, during a difficult season, I changed my email account. I had experienced biblical truth moving from beautiful thought to a living reality through the intersection of personal experience a few times and I believed it would happen again.

Hebrews 11:1 reads, *"Now faith is the assurance of things hoped for, the conviction of things not seen."*

I changed my email to be johnoneagleswings. This is based on Isaiah 40:31 *"but those who hope in the Lord will renew their strength. They will soar on wings like eagles, they will run and not grow weary, they will walk and not be faint."* I chose this new account not because this was my current reality. No, it was a very difficult season. However, I believed it would be true. I based this on previous times when biblical truths had become living realities. I did it to remind myself every time I received or sent an email of a biblical truth that I believed one day would become a living reality. This struggle lasted a few years and then it happened! Physical strength and energy returned. A new normal developed.

What has given your life hope, meaning and strength? If you are a part of a similar faith tradition as mine, has there ever been a time when a Biblical truth intersected with personal experience to create a living reality? Or, shared the experience with another so they may also find some hope, meaning and strength through its telling?

As we prepare for what is next during the Coronavirus pandemic, take time to prepare. Draw upon what gives you hope, meaning and strength, take time to renew your soul by still waters (Psalm 23:2-3) and work as a team and the strength known in friendship and teamwork.

For I believe there will be a time in the future when the biblical truth *"there is a time for every season"* (Ecclesiastes 3:1) will be a living reality as we move from a *"time to weep to a time to laugh"* (Ecclesiastes 3:4) once again…

Attrition: A Chaplain's Perspective on the Pandemic

Attrition: the process of gradually reducing strength or effectiveness of someone or something through sustained pressure.

It is mid-November 2020, the year of the Coronavirus pandemic. I never thought I would use a word like attrition when associated with the medical world. It would seem to fit when talking about a military conflict like World War I. However, 2020, has been unique and challenging and the word attrition seems to fit the reality of everyday life in the hospital.

Let me explain; I work in a hospital in Columbus, Ohio that is a part of a hospital system. This means we have several hospitals and healthcare facilities located throughout the city. Further, this vantage point seems to be reflected throughout the United States and the world. Currently, in the hospital I work in, we have more COVID+ patients admitted in the hospital than at any other time. This number has been consistently rising on a weekly basis and no one knows when this trend might stop. Further, there is less staff available to care for the patients that come our way.

This has occurred for several reasons. First, several departments (including the Spiritual Care department) have had their staff reduced due to the financial struggles medical institutions are experiencing during the pandemic. Second, we have had COVID+ patients for nearly eight months in our hospital. Some staff have gotten tired or overwhelmed and chosen to step away. Many have left due to health concerns for those they love and a knowledge that working in this environment places family and loved ones at a potentially greater risk. Currently, there are 135 staff members within the system who are either quarantined or are COVID+. Many staff members have already had COVID-19 and are trying to work through some of the residual symptoms of the illness; most notably fatigue. Finally, and this is a detail we often try and look away from, more nurses worldwide have died from COVID-19 during the 2020 pandemic than during World War I.[14]

The hospital system I work in has had all the material including PPE (Personal Protective Equipment), ventilators and beds to take care of patients. However, finding enough nurses, PCAs (Patient Care Assistants) and those heroic house cleaners who continually enter COVID rooms is proving to be extremely difficult.

---

[14]   Independent, "COVID nurse death toll now as high as the number of nurses who died during World War One", Tim Wyatt, October 31, 2020.

Attrition. As a world community we are approaching 1.3 million lives lost.[15] What can a chaplain do during such times? What positive impact might we make?

First, and for me this is the most difficult part, we need to admit that we can not be everywhere for everyone. As difficult as it might be the reality is many if not most of the coronavirus patients who die will die alone. This is devastating for families and very hard on staff; including myself. Stating truth with grace and simply being with families and staff in the truth of the moment can be reassuring and healing.

We are approaching one hundred deaths due to COVID in the hospital I work at and I have personally been with twenty-nine families at or near the death of their loved one. It's a lot. It is a lot for staff who have worked on the units for nearly eight months and have no clear vision of an end in sight.

Second, it remains important for the chaplain to model healthy living. This might sound strange; however, the reality is even during hardship, struggle and death there continues to be enormous beauty in the world. In a previous meditation, I mentioned the reality of sacrificial love that can be seen every day. Fall in central Ohio has been especially beautiful with vibrant colored leaves and many days a crisp blue sky. Life continues and life is good!

It is not a time to model a stoic, machismo or even martyr-like demeanor. To confront such tendencies, I have made a conscious practice of encouraging staff to take time away to recharge and enjoy life. During Halloween, I made a habit of

---

[15]   Worldometers.info.coronavirus

asking young parents the costumes and creatures their little ones dressed up as and seeing pictures as often as possible. I am taking the week after Thanksgiving for a time of rest and renewal and I am telling everyone that will listen about my plans. Encouraging them to think about a similar time away.

Finally, when at work and at all times model endurance and hope. This is consistent with my faith tradition. Romans 5:1-5 reads, *"Therefore, since we have been justified by faith, we have peace with God through Jesus Christ. Through him we have also obtained access by faith into this grace in which we stand, and we rejoice in hope at the glory of God. Not only that, but we rejoice in our sufferings, knowing that suffering produces endurance, and endurance produces character, and character produces hope, and hope does not put us to shame because God's love has been poured into our hearts through the Holy Spirit who has been given to us."*

Be smart. Be safe. Be blessed...

R&R (Rest and Reflection)

I have been off work for five days and it is the first week of December 2020. This reflection is different. Most of the time a reflection seems to pour out, complete, only needing a grammar check. This time it has taken five days to get to a place of being able to write and the process of forming thoughts is taking effort.

I have heard of the fog of war and wonder if it relates here. So much has happened in the past month that it is hard to process. So maybe that is the point of this reflection; sorting through all that has happened and finding solid ground.

The week of Thanksgiving was unlike anything I have ever experienced during the pandemic or my twelve-plus years as a chaplain. The number of COVID+ patients in the hospital grew daily and was quickly approaching ninety patients. One hallway that has served COVID+ patients since the beginning had ten deaths in five days. I have personally been with thirty-seven families who have had a loved one die from COVID-19.

In the hospital I work in, the chaplain is called to every patient death. We are to be a compassionate presence who can keep our head in times of intense grief and emotion. We are there to sit with families in the moment and assist with what happens next. These times can be incredibly healing in various ways. There are times families begin telling stories of their loved one, and there are times information and emotional support is given when families are task oriented and want to address the funeral home, care of their loved one and the process that occurs next with Death Certificates etc.. At other times, the chaplain assists by creating space for families at the bedside to have time and a quiet physical space to call other family who many times gather at various times to view their loved one and support each other. Some times families simply chose to sit in silence, there are times families request prayer.

I have been called to be a part of these moments hundreds of times over the years I have worked as a chaplain. It amazes me that I have never had a family request that the chaplain leave. Simply stating in truth my function, "I am Chaplain John and I am here to give some support and help with what happen next," seems to meet a universal human need.

COVID-19 deaths are different. Isolation is the norm and due to this necessity families have not been able to journey alongside a loved one's final earthly journey at the bedside. It is normal for a COVID+ patient to die alone. This is the opposite of what usually happened pre-COVID. Usually a chaplain served to facilitate connections between the patient and their loved one. Many times, this meant sitting with a patient in silence or holding a hand.

Since mid-summer 2020, I have been permitted to enter COVID+ rooms. There is enough Personal Protective Equipment available, and I must follow strict guidelines. I continue to serve the entire hospital and not spreading COVID throughout the hospital must be the primary concern. I can enter rooms for sacramental purposes such as; baptism, communion, praying over a person and administering a Protestant Anointing of the Sick based on James 5:14-15, *"Are any among you sick? They should call the elders of the church and have them pray over them, anointing them with oil in the name of the Lord. The prayer of faith will save the sick, and the Lord will raise them up; and anyone who has committed sins will be forgiven."* In this way, I have entered around a dozen COVID+ rooms. I am amazed at the nurses, personal care assistants, house cleaners and doctors who enter a dozen COVID+ rooms daily.

This said, I am sure the reader is aware that entering a dozen rooms is less than thirty-seven rooms. Therefore, I too, like most families are faced with processing differently and in ways that can present new very challenging hurts that require healing.

We do not know the long-term effect on families who have had to deal with the isolation of their loved and deceased family member. We can expect it may be a different journey and may require unique mental and spiritual care healers to meet the need.

As a chaplain, isolation has forced me to face my own limitations and inadequacies. I think this is the challenge for many if not all healthcare workers who treat COVID+ patients. As hard as I try, the COVID death usually occurs in ways completely opposite to my training and experience. We try our best through phone calls and ZOOM, yet we acknowledge that our best is less than our previous norm.

For healthcare workers, the reality is most patients get better and many continue to die. For those who have served this community since the beginning of the pandemic, the number of deaths only rises. The number of COVID+ patients has not decreased but rather has risen. For nearly four months the number of COVID+ patients in the hospital hovered between twenty-five to forty; then it began to decrease and at one point we only had nine COVID+ patients in the hospital. Last week there were nearly ninety! Further, there is no one who knows if we have reached the peak and when the numbers might begin to decrease. My personal suspicion is that when I return to the hospital next Monday the numbers may have risen.

With all that has been written the reader might be asking, "How could I take a time of rest and reflection at this time?" Some might even believe it to be irresponsible on my part.

To these valid observations I offer my answer. I am a chaplain, therefore, one of my functions is to support staff and model healthy behavior. The moment we think we are indispensable we risk traveling a very dangerous road. Seeking truth and grace, we acknowledge that we serve an *important* role. An important role is not indispensable. As a Christian chaplain I recognize that God is with us.

Knowing that co-workers serve an important role it is imperative I lead by example and model healthy living. Further, I will continue to encourage others to take time for rest and reflection.

In truth, no one knows when the pandemic will end. In truth there are fewer healthcare workers serving a larger group of COVID+ patients. In truth many wonderful healthcare workers have left for a variety of valid personal reasons meaning that many of those treating COVID+ patients are less experienced and younger. In truth it is possible that those experienced healthcare workers who, like me, have been at it since March might be feeling a little worn.

In all these situations it is important to model healthy living. In truth the next few months are going to be rough. In truth whenever we reach that time of relief and new life (whenever that might be, and we look expectantly for a vaccine), it will be important to have as many healthcare workers, colleagues, friends and family prepared for what happens next.

"Remember not the former things, nor consider the things of old. Behold, I am doing a new thing; now it springs forth, do you not perceive it? I will make a new way in the wilderness and rivers in the desert" (Isaiah 43:18-19).

Christmas Eve 2020

"and they shall call his name Emmanuel"
(which means God with us).
Matthew 1:23b

It is Christmas Eve during this strange and challenging year. My wife, who is a Neonatal Intensive Care nurse, is working. All hospitals seem to be struggling to staff their positions and everyone is trying to fill in the best they can. I go to work Christmas morning. I am sitting in the study with the dogs and a cup of coffee. There is a stunningly beautiful snow falling outside.

It has been a strange year. I have never been around this much death and at the same time there have been times when life has been so vibrant. Working in the emergency department seems to represent an incredible contrast in coping. There seems to be an increase in patients who are victims of assault and violence and at the same time I encounter daily reminders of strength, endurance and self-sacrifice rooted in fellowship, hope and faith.

I decided to research my observation and sadly found evidence of increased violence in my city of Columbus, Ohio.

We have tragically broken a record. As of December 24, 2020, there have been 166 homicides in the city.[16] This shatters the previous record of 143 homicides in 2017.[17] As I dug a little further, I discovered that this trend is apparent across the nation. An article in the Christian Science Monitor reported, "This year fifty-one cities of various sizes across the United States saw an average 35% jump in murder from 2019 to 2020."[18] People seem to be struggling with stress, grief, anger, frustration and loss of control during this pandemic year in different ways.

We are a trauma hospital and a number of these victims of violence have been in our hospital. Working with the family anguish during these moments and times is built upon being a compassionate presence who can keep your head. Things can be very confusing and family emotions raw. A chaplain's presence seems to be comforting and a source of calm within the chaos and confusion.

Presence, the gift of being with another. Observing the ways people are coping during this unusual year I have witnessed fellowship, hope and faith contrasted with unhealthy behaviors of increased violence and despair.

This pandemic year has given me a new perspective on Emmanuel (God with us) for there are moments when the most raw and intimate connections are rooted in presence. There are times when grief is so over-whelming that there are no words.

---

[16] Columbus.gov>police-mediarelated

[17] Ibid

[18] The Christian Science Monitor, "2020's murder increase is 'unprecidented.' But is it a blip?", Patrik Johnson, December 14, 2020.

There are times when strength known in self and others can waver. There can even be moments when hope seems to vanish and only presence remains.

If you have ever been around a baby, you may have experienced the calming impact a touch or holding that baby can produce. Words struggle to convey the simplicity and love shared in those moments. Holding the hand of a person nearing death is indescribable; sadness mixed with peace. These have been some of the hardest and holiest moments of my life.

Emmanuel, God is with us. Anyone who has ever had an experience with the Living God knows it changes everything. For even when fellowship and hope have been exhausted there is the lingering echo that there is something more. There is faith that God's presence remains. And slowly, over the course of time, if we have the willingness to see, God's presence is revealed once again. Maybe in the act of another sitting in silence with you, or someone listening to your anger and despair, or holding a hand in prayer.

The advent prayer shared overhead with the hospital has read,

> *O God, it has been an unusual and challenging year. We are living through social unrest and challenges of a global pandemic not known in our lifetime. As we continue to journey through this advent season; a season of expectation and hope, we pause to reflect upon the countless moments of sacrifice for the good of one's neighbor that has*

been such an important part of this unusual and challenging year. We pause to reflect upon all those who have lost a loved one and pray for your comforting presence and assurance that "we will dwell in the house of the Lord forever." Be with us today and every day, Oh Emmanuel, and fill us with childlike joy as we wait expectantly for the gift of love born in a manger and the hope for the world that echoes throughout eternity known in the Christ child. Amen.

Hope, Resolve, Resiliency

"God is the same yesterday, today and forever." Hebrews 13:8

Today is the morning of January 26, 2021. So much has happened in the last month and during this pandemic and I have found these reflections to be personally centering and helpful. Further, I have learned that simply stating truth (with grace), as hard or as unbelievable that truth may be has been healing.

The truth is this: well over two million people have died from the pandemic worldwide; over 400,000 in the United States, and over 10,000 in the state of Ohio. The truth is I am called to all deaths within the hospital (regardless of gestational age), therefore, I am rapidly approaching fifty COVID deaths. These are fifty families that I have been called to provide emotional support and assistance during a time of great despair and loss. The truth is I am fifty-five years old and six of these individuals were younger than me. The Center for Disease and Prevention (CDC) reports over 40,000 people in my age group (55-64) have died from COVID-19 in the United States since the pandemic began less than twelve months ago.

Where is the hope in these unimaginable times? There is hope in the truth! For as horrendous the number of deaths has been the truth is people have NO IDEA how close we came to have the total deaths being two times or three times higher or more. In this way, I know in truth that when I see the number 400,000 in the United States, I know that this number could very easily be 800,000 or 1,200,000 or even higher.

The truth is seen when recognizing that mixed messages about wearing masks was unhelpful and costly in lives. Wearing a mask in the hospital was mandatory before we got our first case. Further, everyone must have their temperature checked every day before entering the hospital. It is not that hard. I have always wondered, if this is a good idea in the hospital then why did it never become the norm at Walmart, Giant Eagle or Target?

There is hope in the truth and the truth is there were four distinct moments in the pandemic journey when the deaths could have VERY easily doubled or tripled or even been worse. The first was at the very beginning when we collectively heard the call to "shelter in place". The purpose was to "flatten the curve" so that we did not overwhelm the medical capacity of a city or region or nation. This shelter in place model worked and many lives were saved!

Further, working where I do, in the middle America city where I live, I cannot state more clearly how close and how real the possibility of being overwhelmed were, as happened in New York and in Italy and Spain. Also, at the very beginning of the pandemic there was no set treatment plan for COVID+

patients. The manual has always been in the writing process during this pandemic because we are journeying together through unknown times.

Second, the truth is that during the summer months of 2020 in the United States the stigma of mass gatherings vanished due to a variety of reasons. This meant that the continued spread of the virus would occur. It meant that the drumbeat of deaths became a drip, drip, drip instead of a furious rush of deaths. Yet, in truth, this also meant that the numbers of deaths would steadily get higher and higher.

The hope during this time was in the many, many lives being saved by medical advances and the heroic daily resolve of healthcare workers. Further, individuals continued to sacrifice for each other daily; most wore masks, many continued to shelter in place, vacations were cancelled or altered. These actions by individuals and communities saved many, many lives!

Third, the November wave. I have never experienced anything like the week of Thanksgiving through the end of 2020. During the week of Thanksgiving, admissions of COVID+ patients rose very quickly and topped over ninety COVID+ patients in the hospital for the first time. There was great anxiety as no one knew when this increase would peak. It would climb to as high as 112 COVID+ patients in the hospital and did not go below ninety until the new year.

It was unlike anything I have ever experienced. The dedication and the resolve of the medical staff. I have personally known dozens of team members who contracted the disease. I remember two events that seem to stand out and represent several. The first was the day when the morgue capacity in the hospital was raised from ten to fourteen. Other hospitals in the city had to resort to ice trucks and we were doing everything we could to avoid that from happening at the hospital I work.

The second instance occurred on a COVID+ unit. I was called to a death that had happened and we were waiting for family to arrive. This is the norm at the hospital, and I was beginning to assist with the decedent care process. As a chaplain I am to be a compassionate presence to staff and listen.

In this situation, I learned that the nurse had just finished school and had recently completed orientation. Later, I learned it was the first patient assigned to her who had died. Then as I watched it quickly became apparent that she had other patients. In fact, I learned her assignment was five non-ICU COVID+ patients! The hospital protocol called for her to gown before entering, gown off before exiting, and then gown on before entering the next room. Every time!

My role was to give support to her, to the family when they arrived and to the entire team who were doing an amazing job supporting each other. The hope was in the abnormal behaviors like this that became normal throughout the hospital and were occurring every day. Many, many lives were saved due to actions like these. Recently, I passed this nurse walking the same unit hallway. She seemed to walk with an added sense of confidence, and I gave her a fist-bump as we passed.

Fourth, is the vaccine. The rapid development of the vaccine can be seen as bordering on a scientific miracle. Further, it is injecting hope that there will be a day when the COVID pandemic is a part of our collective past.

I received my second COVID vaccine last Friday. The vaccine is being distributed at the hospital and the professionalism of those involved with distribution of vaccines to individuals has been amazing. Lives are being saved!

Finally, as I conclude on this late January morning, I am reflecting upon how quickly the abnormal becomes the normal. Throughout January the hospital has ranged between sixty to seventy-five COVID+ patients and we are greatly relieved. How odd it is to say that? We are not repeating the November wave and the sixty to seventy-five COVID+ range now seems manageable by comparison.

How do we begin to return to true "normal" when these types of abnormal have become so commonplace? *God is the same yesterday, today and forever (Hebrews 13:8).* In many ways, the pandemic has reminded us as individuals and communities that the most important things are the most important things.

How would you answer the question concerning "most important things"? Answering that question centers us. It brings us back to normal. *God is the same yesterday, today and forever.* Amen.

A Time to Exhale

Today is the last day of February 2021. The emotions of the hospital are mixed, and I thought it was a good time to try and clear my head.

The emotions within the hospital seem to vary from person to person and floor to floor. There is the obvious grief and exhaustion. In the United States we recently passed 500,000 deaths and worldwide 2,500,000 deaths. At the same time, there is a growing sense of optimism.

On February 9th the hospital dropped under fifty COVID+ patients for the first time since October 2020. On February 24th we dropped under thirty COVID+ patients.

The fear of being overwhelmed is not there at this time and for most of the staff the fear of the virus has lessoned since most of us are now vaccinated. It seems like it is a season to exhale, prepare for what is next, and continue to process all that has happened throughout the pandemic.

Things have happened so fast and in such large numbers that all healthcare professionals and society at large can benefit from the time taken to process. Recently, there were five hundred candles lit and moments of silence held at the White House to simply commemorate and recognize the 500,000 deaths in the

United States. Each individual is connected to others, for no one lives as an island.

A few weeks ago, we had a very difficult death on the COVID floor. All deaths are difficult and at the same time some get under your skin differently since we are all human.

We had our youngest death at the hospital due to COVID to date; age thirty-five. I was not personally involved since it occurred when I was not working. When I returned for my shift at the hospital my role was to listen to staff as they processed and grieved.

While listening I heard a story that I had heard before. It is not uncommon when there is the medical need to put a COVID+ patient on a ventilator for the nurses and medical team to hear what a patient is saying before being placed on the ventilator. I am not in the room during these moments due to space and logistics, so my part is to listen to staff.

These moments can be very difficult. Some patients plead for a sense of reassurance. Some patients verbalize a fear of impending doom. Then the patient is intubated and sedated. Then comes the waiting, as we care for the patient medically, attempt to care for the emotional needs of family, pray and wait. This process can be repeated for days, weeks and on a few occasions' months.

Many times, patients recover. Sometimes patients die and, on a few occasions, the last words spoken by the patient are those that occurred right before intubation. That is a lot of emotional weight to carry for the medical staff and needs to be processed.

I was sick, and you cared for me. Matthew 25:36

A time to exhale. There is a growing recognition that unless there is a COVID variant (something that remains a real possibility) that we may be on the other side of the pandemic. That does not mean everything is suddenly back to "normal" and that people will no longer die of COVD. What it does mean is there is hope in the growing number of people who are vaccinated. There is hope in the continued resolve among healthcare professionals. There is hope in the amazing accomplishments of science. There is hope in communities continuing to sacrifice for the benefit of a neighbor. There is hope in God who gives us what we need to process, grieve, love and begin to dream of new beginnings.

A time to exhale is really a time to process and to prepare for what is next. Whether it is another COVID wave due to a new variant or whether it is the beginning of dreams to be lived out and embraced in a post-COVID pandemic era.

Easter 2021

(Tragedy, Resiliency, Hope)

One of the most difficult things to know at this point in the pandemic is when is it going to end? Everyone wants it to be over though realistically it will be with us a bit longer.

I am writing this reflection the morning after Easter 2021. I worked Saturday night. It is now forty-plus night shifts worked, as a few other chaplains and I, cover the night shifts since pandemic related staff cuts in August. Like many other departments in the hospital, we continue to try and do more with less.

Since Easter 2020 the pandemic has had an impact on everybody's life on the planet. It is not only a local or national experience but also a worldwide experience. Everyone will have a story to tell of their experience of the pandemic.

It has been a tragedy of a magnitude unknown in my lifetime; over 560,000 deaths in the United States and approaching three million worldwide.[19] The numbers are too high to compute. Simplifying the numbers in more comprehensible ways assists us in acknowledging and honoring those who have died.

[19]   Worldometers.info.coronavirus

In my age group 50-64 nearly 78,000 people have died in the United States.[20] I am a sports fan and since I live in Ohio, I like to follow Ohio teams. A visual picture of 78, 000 people would be Cleveland Indians baseball (Progressive Field capacity 35,400), Ohio State basketball (Value City Arena capacity 18,809) and Ohio University football (Peden Stadium capacity 24,000) filled with fans. All these sporting venues filled with cheering fans would be roughly 78,000 people.

Finding accurate figures as to medical workers who have died from COVID-19 is challenging. Since the beginning of the pandemic there has been a difficult balance within the political world and media around information leading to well-reasoned individual decisions and social panic. This said, it is reasonable to state over 20,000 medical professionals worldwide have lost their lives serving others.[21] This would include at least 3584 healthcare deaths in the United States.[22] Over 50% of these healthcare deaths have been in persons under sixty years of age.[23] Further, challenging the narrative that only older people

---

[20] Statista.com, Number of coronavirus disease (COVID-19) deaths in the U.S. as of March 17, 2021

[21] International Council of Nurses press release Geneva, Switzerland, October 28, 2020, *INC confirms 1500 nurses have died from COVID-19 in 44 countries and estimates that healthcare worker COVID-19 fatalities worldwide could be more than 20,000.*

[22] The Staffs of KHN and The Guardian, March 24, 2021, *Lost on the Frontline.*

[23] Ibid.

die of COVID is the reality that hundreds of healthcare workers under the age of forty have died from the pandemic.[24]

The resiliency modeled and sacrifices made by medical professionals and individual citizens continues to astonish and save lives. When I see the death numbers, I know how easily the total deaths could have tripled. In this light it is reasonable to state that individual choices and medical resiliency have saved a million American lives and millions of lives worldwide.

Due to medical advances and incredible medical care at the bedside the mortality rate in the United States is now down to 2%.[25] Sadly, the mortality rate of our neighbor to the south, Mexico, is currently 10%.[26] Thus far in the United States there have been twenty-four million reported COVID cases.[27] A 10% mortality rate would be 2,400,000 in the United States alone.

During the influenza pandemic of 1918, 675,000 died in the United States and an estimated fifty million died worldwide.[28] In the face of the current pandemic, individual choices and medical resiliency have saved millions of lives worldwide!

There is hope in this type of human sacrifice and resolve. Further, the pandemic has re-emphasized how connected we are throughout the world as one human family.

----

[24]   Ibid.

[25]   Worldometers.info.coronavirus

[26]   Ibid.

[27]   Ibid.

[28]   Cdc.gov, *1918 Pandemic.*

Looking to the future through the lens of truth and grace we acknowledge and grieve the tragedy and we honor and celebrate the resiliency and sacrifice. Further, the pandemic is not over and there will be another wave. For some the wave will be a ripple primarily due to the medical miracle of vaccinations, for some it will be a rolling wave and for some a crashing wave. Different places around the world will experience one of these waves.

In the hospital where I work, the number of COVID+ patients has been under twenty for nearly four weeks. One of my sixteen bed units has been completely empty during this time in case there is another surge. For us keeping the number of COVID+ patients under thirty would be a ripple. It would still be significant but not require an expansion from the thirty-two ICU beds designated for COVID patients. Reaching fifty COVID+ patients (like mid-October through mid-February) would be a rolling wave. This would challenge the resources of the hospital. A crashing wave would be seventy or more COVID+ patients (like mid-November through mid-January). During this wave you simply tried to survive and serve. At least for me, that pace and the number of deaths, made it hard to process in the moment.

Tragedy, resilience and hope for in the United States we are seeing the possibility of reaching full vaccination sometime this year. Hope in the responsibility to share and distribute vaccinations throughout the world, especially to the poor and to areas of the world where its residents are economically disadvantaged. Hope in the countless individual sacrifices made by people throughout the world. Hope in the resiliency, sacrifice and resolve of those who seek to serve others.

Yesterday I had the chance to go to church for Easter worship. What a blessing and I remembered last Easter when we were unable to go to church for Easter worship. There is hope.

For Christians there is hope known in the Easter tomb of resurrection. We celebrate that Jesus has risen from the grave. Therefore, a Christian's hope is not found in a human feeling that can come and go. Rather, a Christian's hope is a Living Hope rooted in a Living Lord (I Peter 1:3). Hope in the truth that *'there is a time for every season, and a time for every purpose under heaven"* (Ecclesiastes 3:1). Amen.

Hope

*"Therefore, since we are surrounded by such a
great cloud of witnesses" Hebrews 12:1*

Today is May 17, 2021 and I am writing my last reflection on
my experience as a chaplain during the COVID-19 pandemic.
Over the weekend the CDC (Centers for Disease Control and
Prevention) announced that fully vaccinated people no longer
are required to wear masks indoors. Today it is reported that
37% of the population in the United States is fully vaccinated.
This includes 47.1% of adults over eighteen and 72.6% of adults
over age sixty-five who are fully vaccinated.[29] Earlier today,
President Biden announced that 60% of Americans over the
age of eighteen have received at least one dose of the vaccine.

It is important to note that this does not mean that
COVID-19 has gone away. In the hospital we still have
COVID+ patients, in fact, we had another COVID+ patient
come into the emergency department who was admitted to
the hospital earlier today. What it does mean is that the CDC

---

[29] Npr.org, "How is the COVID-19 vaccination campaign going in your
state?", Updated May 17, 2021 at 9:02 am, Audrey Carlsen, Pien
Huang, Zach Levitt, Daniel Wood.

and the federal government must believe that the possibility of the COVID pandemic overwhelming medical systems, thus resulting in mass causalities and suffering, is behind us.

From the vantage point of the hospital where I serve this assessment seems validated. During the spring surge in 2021, our COVID+ census rose from approximately twenty to around thirty. For us this surge was experienced as a ripple since we did not need to increase the number of assigned COVID beds in the hospital. In fact, for over a month a back-up COVID floor of sixteen ICU beds has been completely empty of patients and staff. It has been held in reserve in case there was a more difficult COVID surge. Today, we are back under twenty COVID+ patients in the hospital.

One of the lessons of the global pandemic is the recognition of how closely we are connected within the human family. Everyone will have a story of their experience of the COVID-19 pandemic. Sadly, during the spring surge there were places like the state of Michigan in the United States, and our southern neighbors in Mexico and Guatemala that experienced a rolling wave challenging the medical institutions in those areas and leading to another increase in daily deaths. Tragically, there are places like India and Brazil that have experienced a tsunami wave of patients this spring that have temporarily overwhelmed the medical capabilities of those countries resulting in thousands of deaths recorded daily.

The pandemic is not over. As of today, nearly, 3,400,000 million people have died of COVID including nearly 600,000 in the United States.[30] And in truth, it is very possible that millions more will die throughout the world due to COVID-19 before the pandemic is truly behind us.

At the same time, there is hope. There is hope in my hospital and throughout the United States that the possibility of medial systems being overwhelmed by COVID+ patients is behind us. In this way, it is hoped that even if COVID will always be here, it will be dealt with in a similar way to the flu, cardiac events or pulmonary issues that are treated and dealt with every day within medical institutions. People will still die of COVID but not at the same rate.

For many, who are fully vaccinated the fear of the pandemic is largely gone. This is true in the hospital. Further, the hope of seeing loved ones, vacations, safely attending weddings, movies, or concerts is returning.

Finally, there is hope that we will live into a new collective understanding of our connectedness as a human family. There is hope that we will work very hard to encourage national governments to share vaccines with nations with fewer resources so that all people can get vaccinated as quickly as possible. There is hope that one day all areas of the world will be able to talk about the COVID-19 pandemic as a memory of the past.

It is not uncommon to be asked how I can deal with so much death. It is a question I have been asked on numerous occasions during the pandemic. To answer this question, I turn to my best teacher on the subject; my mother.

---

[30] Worldometers.info.coronavirus

My mother's father died when she was seventeen years old. I was born when she was twenty-seven. Yet, I do not have a memory of not hearing stories of my grandpa Pfister. There were always pictures of him in the house. There were not enough pictures of him to create a photo album. Listening to those stories I learned of him, who he was and the things he cared about. I also heard stories from my mother of her holding his hand when he breathed his last breath and died. Hearing these recollections removed the fear so many of us experience being that close to death. It also demonstrated the possibility of experiencing moments of the holy during a person's passing from life to life. This holiness can still be felt today in her retelling of the moment of his passing.

I could not do this job if I did not believe there is life beyond this life. Further, I could not keep coming back, day after day, if I did not experience times of holiness at or near the bedside of a dying patient.

These experiences validate my Christian faith for they are living realities of a biblical truth. Hebrews 12:1-2 reads, *"Therefore, since we are surrounded by so great a cloud of witnesses, let us also lay aside every weight and the sin that clings so closely, and let us run with perseverance the race that is set before us, looking to Jesus the pioneer and perfecter of the faith, who for the sake of the joy that was set before him endured the cross, disregarding its shame, and has taken his seat at the right hand of the throne of God."*

Moving from the challenges and despair of the pandemic to dreaming new dreams is difficult. For many, there will remain a time to grieve and we will need to provide support to those who have lost a loved one during the pandemic. It is my hope that the incredible sacrifice of individuals and the many lives lost by medical professionals and support staff will not be forgotten. Perhaps locally or on a national level, there may be a monument or something to remember the incredible sacrifice and commitment of each one in some way, since everyone has their own story of the pandemic.

Recently, I was asked by a very thoughtful young man, "What is the meaning of it all?" I confirmed with him if he really wanted me to answer and he did so I spoke from the heart. To me it is about moments. Moments where we can simply be. Moments when it dawns on us that life really can not get better than this moment. I am blessed to say that these moments in my life include people and experiences of God. I am blessed to have moments and sometimes I wonder how many moments I may have missed due to the worries and business of life. This does not mean the moments were not there. It simply means that I was not present enough at the time to receive the moment as the gift it was meant to be.

If we are blessed to live one of these moments, we then move onto the regular work and challenges of everyday living. Yet, in some strange and beautiful way the memory or echo of the moment never fully goes away. We never know if or when we may experience another moment. However, as a Christian I believe there is always one more. Scripture tells me, *"Do not let your hearts be troubled. Believe in God, believe also in me. In my Father's house there are many dwelling places. If it were not so, would I have told you that I go to prepare a place for you? And if I go and prepare a place for you, I will come again and take you to myself, so that where I am, there you will be also" (John 14:1-3).*

What dreams? What moments may await?

CPSIA information can be obtained
at www.ICGtesting.com
Printed in the USA
BVHW042016021122
650999BV00002B/4